I0190752

GENETICALLY MUTATED CROPS ARE HARMFUL FOR EVERYONE. THE FOOD THAT THEY ARE GROWING IS NOT HEALTHY AND IT HURTS THE ENVIRONMENT TOO.

WHEN WE WERE STUDYING BUTTERFLIES AT SCHOOL, I LEARNED THAT WHEN A BUTTERFLY HATCHES FROM ITS COCOON, IT HAS 20MG OF FAT AND TO MIGRATE THEY NEED TO HAVE 125MG OF FAT. WITHOUT THE FLOWERS, HOW ARE THEY ABLE TO GROW?

THAT IS THE PROBLEM, THEY CAN'T GET ENOUGH FOOD TO LAST THEM FOR THE TRIP THEY NEED TO TAKE ACROSS THE UNITED STATES.

BUT AREN'T THERE OTHER FLOWERS THEY COULD STOP AT ON THE WAY DOWN?

THAT IS WHERE SEVERE WEATHER BECOMES A FACTOR, SUCH AS THE DROUGHTS IN TEXAS. THE STATE'S MILKWEED AND OTHER WILDFLOWERS ARE A VITAL PART OF THE MONARCH'S MIGRATION PATH. THE SEVERE WEATHER KILLS OFF THE WILDFLOWERS. MONARCHS CONVERT SUGAR FROM MILKWEED AND OTHER WILDFLOWERS TO LIPIDS TO HELP FUEL THEIR LONG JOURNEY. WITHOUT FLOWERS, THEY CAN'T GET THE FOOD THEY NEED!

WE FIND LIAM AND JUAN PREPARING FOR THE PRESENTATION.

FINALLY, THIS FARM WOULD BENEFIT EVERYONE IN OUR COMMUNITY AND THAT'S WHY WE WOULD LIKE TO ESTABLISH A COMMUNITY GARDEN NEXT TO OUR SCHOOL.

WHAT DID YOU THINK? DID I LOOK OK?

YOU ARE FORGETTING ALL OF THE DATA ON GARDENING AND SEEDS. YOUR PRESENTATION IS ALL FLUFF. WE NEED TO TELL THEM THE FACTS JUAN.

I USED YOUR FACTS, I JUST DIDN'T USE ALL OF THEM. WE WANT TO KEEP THE AUDIENCE'S ATTENTION BY HIGHLIGHTING KEY POINTS.

MEANWHILE, WARRIOR KALIL IS HAVING A STRUGGLE TOO...
WHAT'S WRONG KALIL?
DIRT
IT'S JUST NO ONE HAD A SPECIAL ASSIGNMENT FOR ME. THEY FORGOT TO EVEN INCLUDE ME. I'M REALLY CREATIVE AND WOULD HAVE LIKED TO DESIGN THE LAYOUT FOR THE GARDEN OR HELP AMELIA WITH THE POWER POINT. THIS ISN'T FAIR.
THEN YOU SHOULD HAVE SPOKEN UP. YOU CAN'T ALWAYS WAIT FOR PEOPLE TO TELL YOU WHAT TO DO. AS WARRIORS, WE NEED TO STAND UP AND GET INVOLVED ON OUR OWN. IF YOU WANT TO USE YOUR TALENTS BETTER, THEN YOU JUST NEED TO SPEAK UP AND LET THEM KNOW.
LIKE WHEN YOU SPOKE UP IN SCIENCE CLASS TODAY? HAHA.
HAHA...VERY FUNNY. SERIOUSLY THOUGH, YOU SHOULDN'T LIMIT YOURSELF TO JUST ART AND DESIGN. BRANCH OUT AND TRY NEW THINGS LIKE LEARNING ABOUT PLANTS AND SOIL. THIS WILL HELP YOU BECOME MORE KNOWLEDGEABLE AND DIVERSE.
I GUESS I COULD HAVE A BETTER ATTITUDE. THIS IS PRETTY COOL.
OK GUYS, LETS GET STARTED!
OK.
MEANWHILE AT BIG CORP INDUSTRIES...
WHAT DID YOU FIND OUT?

The **Meddler** is a wacky scientist who uses his knowledge to manipulate animals and plants. He was one of the Big Corp scientists who worked on Cambio. The Meddler's recent experiments include meddling with seeds and creating genetically modified foods. The chemicals he adds to seeds allows him to enhance the size and look of plants like wheat and corn. However, not known for giving details and being truthful, the Meddler is using chemicals that are harmful to animals, humans and our planet.

www.ingramcontent.com/pod-product-compliance
Lightning Source LLC
Chambersburg PA
CBHW041239020426

42331CB00002B/8